PRECIOUS EARTH

Feeding
the People

Jen Green

Chrysalis Children's Books

First published in the UK in 2004 by
Chrysalis Children's Books
An imprint of Chrysalis Books Group plc
The Chrysalis Building, Bramley Road,
London W10 6SP

ISBN 1 84458 0660

British Library Cataloguing in Publication Data for this
book is available from the British Library.

Editorial Manager: Joyce Bentley

Produced by
Tall Tree Ltd
Designer: Ed Simkins
Editor: Kate Simkins
Consultant: Michael Rand
Picture Researcher: Lorna Ainger

Printed in Hong Kong

Some of the more unfamiliar words used in this book
are explained in the glossary on page 31.

The Publishers would like to thank the following for their
kind permission to reproduce the photographs:

Alamy: Nigel Cattlin 25b, Christine Osbourne 8,
Karen Robinson 23t
Robert Battersby: Tografox 5b, 7b, 11b, 21t, b,
front cover tr, 26
Corbis: Yann Arthus-Bertrand 5t, front cover tl, Bettmann
15b, Jim Erickson 13b, Owen Franken 27b, front cover
bl, Charles & Josette Lenars 4, Minnesota Historical
Society 6, Hans Georg Roth 24, 30, Vince Streano 20,
John Watkins/FLPA 28

Getty Images: Paul S. Howell 9t, front cover c
PA Photos: Ben Curtis 23b
Ed Simkins: 27t
Still Pictures: Philippe Bayle 29, Romano Cagnoni 9b,
Mark Edwards 7t, 10, front cover br, 11t, 14, Paul
Harrison 2, 25t, Philippe Hays 19t, Kim Heacox 17b,
Robert Holmgren 22, Olivier Langrand 15t, A.
Riedmiller 19b, 31 Cyril Ruoso 16, Sean Sprague 12,
UNEP 1, 18, back cover, Martin Wyness 13t

Contents

Feeding the world

All the food we eat comes from plants and animals. Growing crops and rearing animals for food is known as agriculture, and it is the biggest industry in the world.

Farming began over 10 000 years ago, as people began keeping animals in herds and raising crops. Early farmers saved the best seeds to sow the following year, and so gradually crops improved. For centuries, farmers have changed the landscape to make it more suitable for growing crops.

▼ *Farming dates back thousands of years. This painting from about 1200 BC shows an ancient Egyptian farmer harvesting crops with a sickle (a curved blade).*

Over the last hundred years, the world's population has grown very rapidly. So farmers have had to grow more food. In recent years, farmers in rich countries have produced big harvests using modern methods and equipment. However, these methods also have drawbacks. They can harm wildlife, cause pollution and exhaust the soil.

▲ A modern combine harvester can harvest a huge field of wheat in a few hours.

CLOSE TO HOME

In rich countries, most people now buy nearly all their food from supermarkets. These shops have a major influence on the food we eat. Supermarkets stock a huge range of foods – usually around 40 000 different products.

Advances in farming

Methods have improved steadily since farming began. Progress has been particularly rapid in the last 50 years. However, these changes have not always been good for the natural world.

Just a century ago, farming was very different in rich countries. Farms often had small fields bordered by hedges, and most farmers reared both crops and animals. Animals pulled farm equipment. In the mid-twentieth century, petrol-driven tractors replaced animals. Hedges, which sheltered wild plants and animals, were torn up to make fields bigger, so machines could move about easily.

▼ An early steam-driven tractor pulls a plough in Midwestern USA around 1915. Petrol-driven tractors soon replaced steam-driven ones.

◄ Important foods, such as wheat and rice, originally from just one region are now grown in many areas. Here potatoes, originally from South America, are being collected in India.

From the 1950s, scientists developed new varieties of crops, such as wheat and rice, that produced bigger harvests. This was called the Green Revolution. Instead of growing many different crops, farms began to specialise in fewer crops or just one. However, growing the same crop year after year removes too much nourishment from the soil, so farmers had to use chemical fertilisers.

CLOSE TO HOME

Hedges are home to many wild animals and plants. The hedge itself is made of woody shrubs, such as blackthorn, along with climbers, such as ivy and brambles. Use a field guide to identify shrubs in a country hedge. The more different kinds there are, the older the hedge.

Water for farming

All plants and animals need fresh water to survive, so water is vital for farming. Agriculture uses far more water than any other industry – over 70 per cent of the world's fresh water supplies.

Around 5000 years ago, Middle Eastern farmers learned to water, or irrigate, their crops using river water. Today, water for irrigation is taken from rivers and lakes and also from underground water sources. Irrigation is widespread, but it can cause the soil to become too salty for farming.

◄ *The shaduf was one of the earliest machines invented to collect water. It is still used in countries, such as Egypt, today.*

In recent years, scientists have developed several new, efficient ways of using water in farming. Hydroponics (shown here) is a method of growing crops without soil, by rooting plants in mineral-rich water, sand or gravel.

▼ *In rich countries, modern irrigation systems use huge quantities of water. Much of the water is wasted: it drains away or evaporates into the air before reaching the crop.*

In some places, water is scarce, and crops die in long, dry periods called droughts. Dams are built to store water for irrigation and also to generate electricity. However, dams destroy wild land and can often force people out of their homes.

Poor farmers

In poor parts of the world, including Africa, Asia and South America, many people still use traditional methods for farming. Most farmers cannot afford chemical fertilisers or machinery, such as tractors, so the amount of crops harvested is often small.

Many farmers in poor countries can only grow enough food to feed their families. This type of farming is called subsistence farming. Elsewhere, governments encourage farmers to grow cash crops, such as sugar, tea, cotton and coffee, for sale abroad. These crops travel huge distances to be sold in the supermarkets of rich nations. The foreign supermarkets make large profits, but local farmers earn very little.

◄ *In poor countries, the hard work of farming is often done by hand or using simple tools. Planting rice seedlings in muddy fields is tiring, back-breaking work.*

From the 1960s and 70s, the "supercrops" of the Green Revolution have helped some farmers in poor countries to increase their harvests. However, the new crops aren't successful everywhere. In some areas, they do not suit the soil or the local climate. They often require chemical fertilisers or pesticides, which poor farmers can't afford.

◄ *Crops for sale abroad are often grown on large plantations like this one in Malaysia. This worker is harvesting a milky sap called latex, which is used to make rubber.*

CLOSE TO HOME

Much of the food we buy in supermarkets comes from poor countries. Many products are now labelled to show where the food was grown.

Feast and famine

Everyone needs nourishing food and a varied diet for the body to grow and stay healthy. However, millions of people die each year through starvation or illness caused by a poor diet.

Around the world, farmers now grow enough food for everyone, but the food is not evenly distributed. Often, it is not in the right place at the right time. In poor regions, such as Africa, one in every five people goes hungry. Drought, war and disasters, such as hurricanes and floods, bring famine – widespread hunger – when many people starve.

◄ *In recent years, Sudan in East Africa has been hit by several terrible famines. Millions of people, like this child, survive on emergency food aid.*

In rich countries, food is often so plentiful that many people waste it and also overeat. Eating too much makes people overweight and at risk of illness, such as heart disease. If farming and world food stocks were better managed, more food would get to the people who need it.

In recent times, rich countries have sometimes grown so much food that the surplus builds up to form "mountains" like these bags of potatoes. You might think that the extra could be used to feed starving people, but the cost of transporting the food before it spoils is often too high.

◀ *In the United States (where these men live), half of the population is overweight, while less than 4 per cent don't have enough to eat. In India, the figures are reversed.*

Lost land

Farmland already covers a massive one-third of Earth's land area. This includes nearly all the areas of more fertile soil. To feed the growing numbers of people, some of the wild lands that remain may have to become farmland.

In some areas, farming the land too much has done lasting damage. For example, too many cattle or sheep grazing on a small pasture can strip all the vegetation. Then the bare soil dries up and can wash away in heavy rain or blow away on the wind.

▼ In dry parts of Africa, goats, sheep and cattle can easily graze pastures bare. In some places, overgrazing has turned fertile land into desert.

▲ Beef cattle graze an area of cleared rainforest in Madagascar. Rainforests in many places are being cut down to meet rich countries' demand for beef.

As human populations grow, so more food is needed. One way of meeting the need is to grow crops on more wild land. Every year, forests, grasslands and wetlands are destroyed to create new farmland. Wild plants and animals lose their homes.

LOOK CLOSER

In the 1930s, modern farming methods brought disaster to the American Midwest. Farmers ploughed up the natural grasslands there to grow crops. But the bare soil turned to dust after several years of drought, then high winds blew it away. The whole area became a barren "Dustbowl", and huge areas of land were abandoned. The damage took years to repair.

Chemicals and farming

In the last 50 years or so, many farmers have increased their harvests by using chemicals to kill pests and fertilise the soil. When these chemicals are carried away by rivers or blown by the wind, they pollute the natural world.

Fertilisers provide the nutrients crops need to grow. They are vital on farms where the same crops are grown year after year. Farmers also spray their fields with poisons called pesticides to kill weeds, insects and fungi that cause disease. The poison spreads through the natural world, as small creatures eat sprayed plants, and larger animals eat the smaller animals.

▲ *A tractor sprays pesticide on crops in France.*

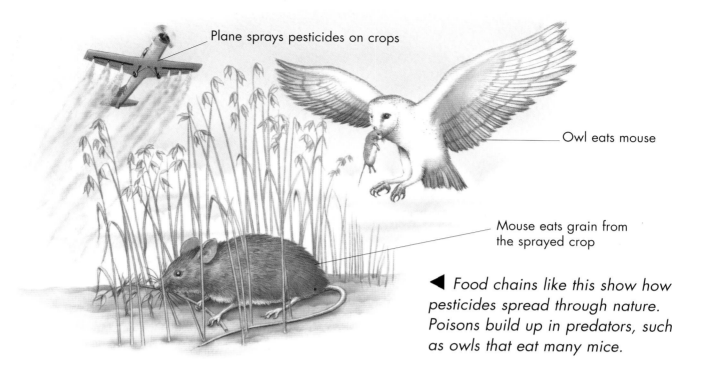

Plane sprays pesticides on crops

Owl eats mouse

Mouse eats grain from the sprayed crop

◀ *Food chains like this show how pesticides spread through nature. Poisons build up in predators, such as owls that eat many mice.*

When fertilisers drain off the land into rivers and lakes, they cause tiny water plants called algae to spread through the water. Too much algae can block the light and also use up the water's oxygen. This harms fish and other water life. Chemicals from farming can also pollute drinking water.

LOOK CLOSER

From the 1950s, a powerful pesticide called DDT was used to kill insects. No one realised that the poison would harm wildlife. Cropland predators, such as owls, absorbed the poison. This weakened the shells of the eggs they laid, so that their chicks failed to hatch.

Farm animals

For thousands of years, farm animals, such as cattle, pigs, sheep and chickens, have been reared for meat, milk, wool and eggs. Now some farmers are using modern methods to produce more food.

In ancient times, farmers wandered from place to place to find grazing for their sheep, goats or cattle. Later, farmers grazed their herds in fields. Now some farmers rear their animals indoors in sheds or pens, rather than letting them roam outside. They argue that this method, called factory farming, helps to produce cheap food, but many people think it is cruel.

▼ *Factory-farmed chickens are reared in tiny cages with no space to move.*

Animals reared on factory farms are given food containing hormones – chemicals that make them grow rapidly. Disease can spread quickly, so the animals are also given medicines called antibiotics to prevent illness. However, eating meat containing antibiotics or hormones can make people ill.

▲ These people are protesting against the practice of transporting farm animals long distances for slaughter. The animals are often transported in cramped and dirty conditions.

LOOK CLOSER

The beef, bacon, lamb, chicken or pork we buy at supermarkets all come from animals reared on farms. It costs much more to produce meat than it does to grow crops.

From field to shelf

Much of the food that we buy from supermarkets has been changed in some way to make it last longer or look or taste better. However, this produces waste and pollution and can even harm our health.

Much of the fresh food produced by farms is frozen, dried or treated in some way to preserve it. Chemicals called additives are added to many foods to stop them spoiling or to add colour or flavour. These chemicals can cause health problems, such as allergies, particularly in children.

▼ These oranges are being loaded on board a ship for transport to supermarkets. Transporting food across the globe uses huge amounts of fuel, and the burning of fuel pollutes the environment.

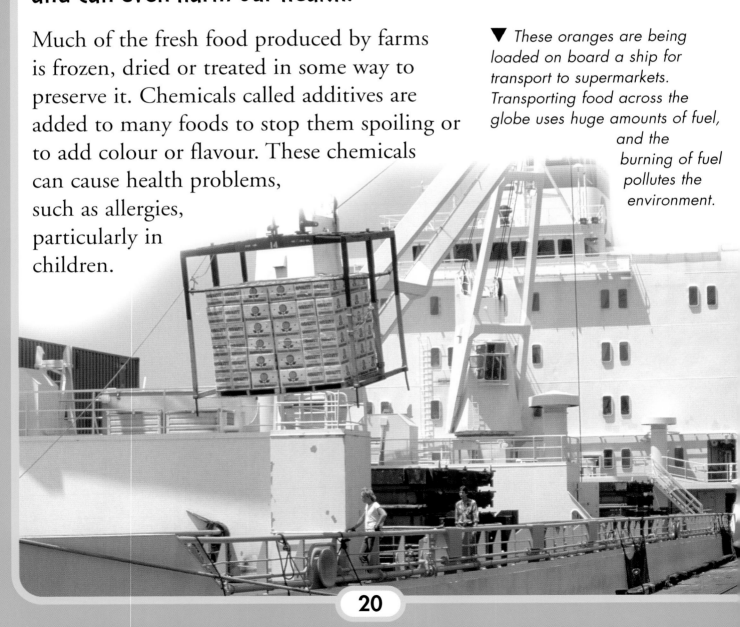

◀ Cereals, biscuits and other foods may have several layers of unnecessary packaging. Fast foods use lots of packaging, too.

Most food in supermarkets is packaged in cartons, cans and other containers to keep it fresh and also make it more attractive. However, this packaging is just thrown away later. Materials such as plastic and glass don't decay and are difficult to get rid of.

CLOSE TO HOME

Most foods in your fridge or kitchen cupboards have been preserved in some way, either by freezing, smoking, drying, pickling, canning or using additives.

Changing nature

For centuries, farmers have produced new types of crops by breeding from plants with the best qualities. Now scientists can produce new crops quickly, by changing their genes. These crops are said to be genetically modified (GM for short).

Inside the cells of all living things are tiny structures called genes, which control inheritance. Scientists can now mix genes from two different living things to produce new types of plants and animals. Crops can be grown to look or taste better or to cope better with drought, frost or pesticides.

▲ *These tomatoes have had their genes changed to make them stay fresher for longer and to improve their flavour.*

Some experts say that GM crops could produce big harvests to feed starving people. However, many people feel that more testing is needed to make sure GM crops are safe. They worry that GM crops could cause health problems or spread to change the genes of other plants.

▲ *These protesters are destroying a field of GM crops because they believe they are dangerous.*

LOOK CLOSER

Scientists have also been able to change genes to produce clones – exact copies – of animals, such as this sheep. In the future, cloning could allow farmers to improve their animals, but some people think that cloning is wrong.

Organic farming

Organic farming is a method of farming that does not use chemicals. A growing number of farmers in rich countries are returning to more natural methods.

Organic farms use traditional methods to fertilise the soil and protect crops from pests. Fields can be fertilised with compost, animal manure (dung) or seaweed instead of chemicals. The practice of crop rotation, whereby different crops are grown in the fields each year, also helps to nourish the soil. So does planting two different crops, such as wheat and beans, side by side.

▼ *Hedges on traditional farms like this one in Portugal provide homes for wildlife. Organic farmers don't destroy hedges and may even plant more.*

◀ *Free-range chickens and other animals are not given feed containing chemicals.*

CLOSE TO HOME

Organic farmers use natural methods to control crop-eating insects. In the wild, ladybirds feed on aphids that damage plants. Farmers can attract the ladybirds by planting certain flowers. This natural method of pest control also works in the garden.

Organic farmers who rear animals allow them to roam freely. Milk, meat and eggs produced in this way are called free-range. Organic methods sometimes produce less food and require more labour. This makes organic food a little more expensive, but many people are happy to pay more for chemical-free and cruelty-free food.

How can we help?

We can all help to encourage farming methods that don't harm nature, through the choice of the food we buy. We can also help poor farmers by buying fair-trade foods.

Encourage your family to buy locally grown food from farms, shops and markets. Some areas have box schemes, through which organic farms supply boxes of fruit and vegetables to homes each week. Supermarkets now stock organic foods, which are better for both you and nature. In supermarkets, look out for foods that have been grown locally rather than transported across the world.

▲ *Much of the rubbish we throw out each week can be used again. Take it to a recycling centre rather than putting it in the bin.*

▲ Look out for fair-trade products like the ones shown here.

▼ Local fruit, vegetables and cheese are sold at farmers' markets. Buying food here supports local farmers and helps to reduce the pollution caused by transporting food long distances.

Avoid heavily packaged foods that create waste. How much waste does your family recycle? Bottles, tins, cartons, plastic trays, newspapers and clothes can all be taken to recycling centres, so the materials can be used again.

Find out about and support charities that protect nature or supply food aid to poor countries. You could do a sponsored walk, run, swim or another activity to raise money for your favourite charity.

Try to buy fair-trade products, which many supermarkets now sell. These foods give growers in poor countries a fair share of the profits made by selling the food.

Projects

Gardeners as well as farmers can achieve good results without harming nature. Become a green gardener by following the hints below. Try the experiment on page 29 to find out how plants absorb nourishment from the soil.

BE A GREEN GARDENER

Like organic farmers, green gardeners fertilise the soil and protect plants from pests without using chemicals. Here's how it's done.

▲ *Frogs eat insect pests, including slugs. Encourage frogs to live in your garden by having a small pond.*

1. A compost heap can be made using four posts and wooden boards. Ask an adult to help you. Put garden waste and kitchen peelings on the heap. Turn it over now and then with a fork to allow air inside. Now spread the well-rotted compost on the soil and dig it in.

2. Slugs and snails are a pest in gardens. Keep them at bay by encouraging birds, their natural enemies. Put out crumbs, nuts and bacon rind to attract birds. Don't use slug pellets on the garden, because they poison birds.

3. Water is precious. Don't waste it in the garden. Sprinklers and hoses use huge amounts of water. Use a watering can instead filled from a rain barrel. Water plants in the evening, not during the day when it is sunny.

INVESTIGATING PLANTS AND NUTRIENTS

Find out how plants absorb water and nutrients by putting white flowers in a jar of water with some food colouring.

1. Half fill a clear glass vase or jar with water. Put some white flowers, such as daisies or carnations, in the vase or jar.

▼ *Crops and wild plants on farms absorb nourishing minerals in the same way that flowers suck up water through their stems.*

2. Add a few drops of food colouring. You can buy this from most supermarkets.

3. After several hours, you'll see the petals change colour as the plants suck up water through their stems.

CAMPAIGN GROUPS

WWF
Panda House, Weyside Park, Godalming,
Surrey GU7 1XR
Website: www.wwf.org.uk

Friends of the Earth
26–28 Underwood Street, London N1 7JQ
Website: www.foe.co.uk

Greenpeace
Canonbury Villas, London N1 2PN
Website: www.greenpeace.org

Oxfam
Oxfam House, 274 Banbury Road, Oxford, OX2 7DZ
www.oxfam.org.uk

WEBSITES

Compassion in World Farming: www.ciwf.co.uk

Food and Agriculture Organization of the United Nations (FAO): www.fao.org

Soil Association, Britain: www.soilassociation.org.uk

Organic Consumers Association, North America: www.organicconsumers.org

US Environment Protection Agency: www.epa.gov/students

Environmental Investigation Agency: www.eia-international.org

New Scientist Planet Science page: www.newscientist.com

Factfile

• Over half of all the people in the world do farm work of some kind. More than 2.5 billion people worldwide earn their living by farming.

• Crops, such as potatoes, corn (maize), rice and rubber, were unknown in Europe until fairly recent times. Explorers brought them back from newly discovered lands, and now they are grown in suitable climates around the world.

• Grain crops, also called cereals, are the world's most important food crops. They include wheat, barley, rice, oats, corn, millet and sorghum. Cereal crops are grown on about one-sixth of the world's farmland.

• On factory farms that produce eggs, up to 10 000 hens may be kept in a single shed. The birds receive food and water from machines. Eggs drop down chutes ready to be collected.

• So much underground water has been pumped up from beneath Mexico City in North America that the ground and the buildings on it have sunk up to 2m in places.

• In the USA, nearly half of all grain crops, such as wheat and corn, are used to feed farm animals. Huge quantities of grain are needed to fatten beef cattle to produce a relatively small amount of meat.

Glossary

Cell
The tiny structures from which all living things are made.

Cereal
One of a variety of grain crops, including wheat, rice, oats and barley.

Evaporate
To change from water into water vapour.

Famine
Widespread hunger caused by poor harvests.

Fertilise
To add manure or certain chemicals (fertilisers) to the soil to make it good for growing crops.

Genes
Tiny structures inside the cells of living things that are responsible for passing on traits, such as hair colour, from parents to their young.

Genetically modified (GM)
Foods that have had their genes changed by adding genes from a different species.

Green Revolution
The introduction from the mid-twentieth century of new crop varieties that produced big harvests.

Hydroponics
A modern method for growing crops without soil.

Irrigation
The watering of the land using water taken from a river or lake or from an underground well.

Nutrients
Nourishing chemicals that plants need to grow.

Organic farming
Growing crops and rearing animals without using chemicals.

Pesticide
A chemical used to kill pests, such as weeds and harmful insects.

Subsistence farming
When farmers are only able to grow enough food to feed their families, with little left over to sell for profit.

Wetlands
Any body of fresh water, including streams, rivers, lakes, ponds, swamps, marshes and bogs.

Index